Table of Contents

Chapter 1: Doubling Your Business.. in Half the Time
Chapter 2: Never, Ever Get a Bad Customer Again
Chapter 3: Never Lose a Sale
Chapter 4: Never Run Out of Leads
Chapter 5: No More Inefficiencies in Your Business
Chapter 6: The Rocket is Launching… Are You Ready?

Chapter 1: Doubling Your Business.. in Half the Time

Imagine a world where all entrepreneurs were inspired, impactful, inspirations, leaders, and problem solvers. However, the problem entrepreneurs face that prevents them from living in this world is that they struggle, and instead of being the rocket to their dream, their business is a sinking ship to their worst nightmare. This is the story of how a regular guy went on a remarkable journey to transform his sinking ship to a rocket, from being in debt and overworked, to earning more than $375,000 in 1 year, working half the time and touching more lives. The principles and strategies in this book will allow you to find the fuel to turn your business into your rocket as well.

Who can benefit the most from this book? If you're a solopreneur or an entrepreneur with a small team, and you work with information, expertise, technology, services, training, coaching, consulting or education, and you're doing anywhere within $100,000 revenue in the past 12 months, you will benefit the most out of this book. Even if you're not, whether you're thinking of starting your business, or perhaps you've gone past the 6 figure mark, you will still find many principles and strategies that can help you towards your goals.

The problem with so many business owners I meet is they started their business with the objective to have a lot more income, a lot more impact, and have a life of freedom to be able to take care of their family, but they are feeling stuck in their business. They are not generating enough cash flow, always worried about how to get the next customer or the next contract, and they're worried about how to grow their business so that they have peace of mind, and finally remove themselves from it and finally have freedom.

When you achieve this in your business, you go from cash flow anxiety to cash flow confidence, from constant firefighting to freedom, and from being a best kept secret to having a million dollar message. How would your life and business change if you were able to achieve this for yourself? Would this change something in your business, or could this change possibly *everything*?

I'm lucky to say that today as long as I have an internet connection in my laptop or my phone, I can run my business. In fact, if you look at the picture below, you would see that this was my office by the beach in Da Nang, Vietnam. I spent 2 weeks early in 2015 working from its beaches - in fact, in that year we worked around Bali, Kuala Lumpur, Bangkok, Istanbul, New York, Florida, Sydney and the Caribbean. And it's something that I want so many entrepreneurs to be able to achieve and experience - growing their business to impact so many more lives and have the freedom of choice.

Working by the beach in Da Nang, Vietnam - January 2015

But it wasn't always this way. In fact, if you saw me two years ago at

Christmas 2013, you would have found me in the penthouse office or one of the nearest office buildings in Kuala Lumpur, Malaysia where I was spending Christmas evening working on a 100-page proposal for the Malaysian government. At that point in time, I was overworked. I was really stressed because I was constantly worrying about how to get more clients and cash for my business. We were broke, in debt and the worst part was that I was working 16 hour days, 7 days a week and was sacrificing my house, my loved ones, my relationships, my hobbies and my passions. I worked in the office all the way until New Year 2014 and sadly we didn't get the contract. Does any of this sound familiar to you? Do you find yourself sacrificing, working hard and not getting the results that you want in your business? If so, please listen to my story and how I got out of this.

Overworked, overweight, and broke on Christmas evening 2013 in Kuala Lumpur, Malaysia

At that point in time, we were $50,000 in debt, and I had no idea how I could get out of it but I knew that I had to make a change. I had to make a change both in my life and in my business. Because whatever that brought me at that point could not get me out. So I decided that I would change. I left that business partnership and I decided to focus on Street Smart University, my company, and within a few weeks someone came to me and asked me to build them a website and run their online marketing campaign. At first, I said no. But they said they could pay me $11,000 for the contract.

If you were in my shoes, and you had $50,000 in debt and were struggling to get more cash and clients, what would you do? I said yes and I decided to have a business that focused just doing this and we grew that web consultancy business to more than $125,000 in revenue within six months in the second half of 2014. This was great because this absolutely turned around my fortune and got me out of the hole that I had built for myself.

However, there was a problem. We were still working really hard, 12 to 14 hours a day, 6 days a week. I constantly had to be on the phone, Skype, or email with my clients, with my development team, with my sales team. I had clients calling me up at 1 a.m. and asking me for urgent things or complaining to me about things that weren't to their liking, and the worst part was many clients did not value me. They didn't see the expertise and the value that we brought to them and they compared us to a cheap overseas freelance developers. If you're not spending time with ideal clients, then perhaps you may know this pain as well.

That was when I met a remarkable man. He turned out to be a business coach. When I met him I didn't know he was an Amazon bestselling author, a multi-millionaire serial entrepreneur, international speaker and business growth hacker. Christopher Duncan saw the potential in me and my business. He started to partner with me and had been my mentor at the start of 2015. But first, we had to agree to pay him $60,000 to be our business coach, so he could help us explode our business.

If you are a small business owner like we were at that time, you would know that you won't have that kind of money just sitting in the bank. It was a difficult decision, but we decided to work together. Within two and a half weeks of working together, we created an event in Singapore where we had 42 people in the room, and at the end of it, we made more than $46,000 of revenue in business coaching programs. This was absolutely mind-blowing for me because I spent months after months chasing clients one by one, sending them emails, calling them, meeting them for a few thousand dollars contract. This was a huge thing because we made so much more money in very little time - just one day of an event, with two and a half weeks of preparation.

After 10 years of business mistakes, thousands upon thousands of dollars of investments into learning and setting up the business and many painful lessons, finally all of it started clicking together for me. Wouldn't it be cool if you could do the same for yourself? What if you could generate a lot more revenue for your business in half or less the time, reach more people, and allow yourself to have a lot more time for your loved ones and doing the things that mattered to you?

My business partner, Fazil (left), myself, and my mentor Christopher Duncan (centre), at the end of 3 months and $250,000 revenue.

We grew it even further in the next 3 months, generating more than $250,000 in revenue within the first 3 months of working with our coach. This was amazing for me, it doubled our results in half the time, and as an added benefit, we really started to work with our ideal customers who loved us for who we were, took less of our time and valued our expertise. We had a lot more time to be able to relax, have time to also take care of our loved ones and travel, ending up in more than 12 countries in 2015.

Besides growing our business, we started getting attention from the media. In the past 2 years, we have gotten more than 20 media features for our company and partners. We were featured on television, radio, newspapers, magazines, online and offline in regional events. We got to the semi-finals of Startup@Singapore and Echelon Asia, the 2 largest business startup competitions in the region. These created even more opportunities, exposure and credibility for us.

Features in multiple media platforms.

Coming from a place where I was in debt to doing multiple 6 figures in business in less than a year, I was inspired to go out and help other people as well. The problem was, most entrepreneurs and small businesses would struggle to get leads, and this was because they would not have a client tap that they can switch on, on demand, to generate leads, clients and cash. Their client tap is dry.

Knowing this was the biggest problem for businesses, I put all my experiences, knowledge and previous failures and successes into a system called the Fast Business Growth. These are the three steps that any entrepreneur or small business owner in any industry can implement to experience tremendous growth in less time.

The Fast Business Growth System - 3 Proven Steps To Add 6 Figures To Your Business.

The Fast Business Growth System has three steps. The first is Target. Do you have a target customer? When you have your target defined, it would be so much easier to hit it.The first thing I learned in growing any business was to find the most profitable customer, target them and communicate with them to become paying clients.

The second step in the system is Trap. In the case of an entrepreneur wanting to impact many more lives, you need to have a trap. It is the way capture all your leads. This is your online asset which markets for you 24/7 so you don't have to.

Do you have a bucket to trap all your leads, or is your bucket leaking? Some entrepreneurs don't even have a bucket set up, and they wonder why they don't get more leads! This step talks about your online websites and systems. You need to have a well-built trap which not only captures the leads coming in, but also to build a relationship with your customer so that even before they meet you or talk to you they are already educated on their problem, what the ideal solution is for them, and why your product is the best fit, and thus they come to you hungry for your solution.

The last step in the system is Traffic. It is the ability to generate massive numbers of exposure and leads into your business because growth depends on predictable leads coming into your business. The second thing that I learned that I put into the system is the ability to get your business, your brand and your name to so many people in the market using at least 7 techniques which I will share with you below. It's important to not only have quantity of leads, but quality leads as well. The leads which are qualified, which are part of the target market, and who know you, like you and want to work with you.

When these three steps are done correctly, you are able to bring 6 figures into your business. I learned how to systemise everything so that you can create predictable results for yourself. Systems are needed so that you can predictably generate results, scale up your business and finally remove yourself from your business. This is how I created the systems with which I'm teaching you right now. My books, websites, videos and programs allow me to deliver a lot more value to a lot more people, and many more things happen in the background so that I reach more people, with much less of my time. This is what will allow you to reach a big vision and achieve freedom.

Know that what I teach you is not 100% created by me. I've learned from some true greats, from Christopher Duncan, Anthony Robbins, Andy Harrington, Kane Minkus, T Harv Eker, and many more great teachers and role models. In fact, I spent more than 10 years and $100,000 on my own education, learning and development which you don't have to. You don't have to go through the pain, the investment and the time which I went through to achieve the same results in your business. The system I've put together is such that you just have what works right now, not just for me, but also to successful and growing companies around the world in different industries.

What you're looking to build for your business is a system, because systems deliver results which are predictable. Systems are scalable and can be automated so that you don't have to be in the business for the business to run. Sounds good?

So this is the high level overview of three step Fast Business Growth system, the fastest way you can target, trap and generate traffic your way to adding 6 figures to your business in the next 12 months. When you do this, you achieve client certainty, cash flow confidence, freedom and having a million dollar message sent across so you can finally be that million dollar entrepreneur you want to be.

I want this experience in this book to be interactive, so before we get into the key points of the system I would like you to start looking at yourself, your business and conduct a self-assessment. Looking at Target, Trap and Traffic, out of 10, where are you now? 0 being non-existent and 10 being the absolute ideal.

In terms of Target, do you have an ideal customer profile? The second thing that you want to do is to look at your Trap. Do you have educational videos, a website which builds your client list and converts leads into calls, purchases or consultations? In Traffic, are you getting a lot of traffic to your assets, or is traffic generation a guessing game for you?

I'd like you to give yourself the score of where you are in your business, because this gives you a base from which you can focus on. It is likely that improving one or more of these areas over the next few months with the right guidance is where you can really put your business on steroids and get the results you want this year.

Self - Diagnosis

TARGET	? / 10
TRAP	? / 10
TRAFFIC	? / 10

We're now going to move fast into the real meat of the system where you have actionable steps and ideas which you can execute in your business. I hope you're ready. I'll see you in the next chapter.

Chapter 2: Never, Ever Get a Bad Customer Again

In this chapter, we would go through the first step of the system, Target. This step answers the questions, "How do I get more clients? How can I not work with horrible clients? How can I know where and when my next client will come? How do I define my ideal client?" Answering these questions correctly will allow you to never, ever get a bad customer again and for you to just work with the ideal customers who love and respect you.

Identify your ideal client with laser focus

Why is having an ideal client important? If you're a business owner, you may be familiar with the feeling of going out to talk to a lot of people about your business. Maybe you went to a networking session and gave your business card to as many people as possible and tried to follow up with them for a meeting. Perhaps you spent lots of time, money and energy doing it to realise not all the people you met with for coffee, probably even up to 90% of them, were potential clients. Only 10 to 20% of them would actually buy anything. That's because the vast majority of people you would meet at a general event are not your target market. They are not interested or are unaware of the problem that you can help solve. The ability to sieve through the market fast and finding ideal clients is what will grow your business fast.

So if you don't have an ideal client defined yet, then you would only end up talking to everyone, using a lot of energy and spending a lot of time and money for very little return. What you want to do right now is to define your ideal customer with laser focus and precision. How does one do this?

First, we need to understand how to define an ideal customer. Most entrepreneurs would tell me they do have an ideal customer. When I question them more, they realise that they actually have no idea. So here are some of the things that you want to have when you define an ideal customer:

- Gender, age, background
- Profession
- Location
- The biggest problem that they're looking at
- The biggest aspiration that they have
- The frustrations that they're facing right now
- The biggest fears that they face
- The biggest desires that they have and
- The biggest unmet need that they have that no one else is solving for them

You need to understand their psychology. That means what do they think about themselves? They might think of themselves as hardworking or lazy. Do they think of themselves as smart or not so smart? How about sporty or studious? This makes a huge difference to understand the ideal customer and how you need to communicate with them and where you will find them. Realize that when you define your ideal customer, it becomes obvious where you should look for them. For example, if your ideal customers are parents, then perhaps you should start looking at parenting websites, parenting forums, parenting events. If you are looking at students as your ideal customer who are in college, then you want to start looking at job fairs, career fairs, education fairs. So where you find a customer, how you communicate with them and how you describe their problems and needs all rest on how you define your ideal customer

So how does one do this? Firstly, you need to have an idea who the ideal customer is. Perhaps you want to talk to business owners. Within the market of business owners, you would want to look at 30 to 40-year old business owners. I would recommend you to look at 10 year age ranges because beyond 10 years is hard to find commonalities.

A 30-year old man would not have the same language, priorities, concerns and thoughts as a 50-year old man. They are in different phases of life and have different experiences. A 30-year old business owner would have much more in common to a 39-year old business owner. This is why you want to keep it within an age range of 10 years. When you have decided your age range, go out and talk to your customer. Identify five people that fall into this category, call them and offer to buy them coffee or have a casual chat with them. Ask them a list of questions which give you the description of what we have detailed above.

Make sure you record or transcribe everything from the interview because this is valuable to you. This is the market research that would save you a lot of time, effort and money in your business. When you have transcribed every interview, you would start to look at the commonalities between all the interviews, then put them into the target profile. Your target profile should be just one page, identifying who is your ideal customer.

Give this ideal customer a name. Place all the information into one page where you can find them handy. This becomes your go-to guide whenever you speak to your customer online, offline, face to face, on the phone, in brochures or in events. It is really important that you don't use marketing jargon or industry lingo. Use the language of your customer. The principle behind all of this is that you speak to your ideal customer, get the exact language in their head, and then you feed it back to them in everything you say, do or create. This allows you to have a laser focus on your ideal customer profile which then you can use to generate a lot of money in your business and help a lot more people. If you're not focused on your ideal customer and try to talk to everyone, you become generic, bland and lost in the market.

The powerful techniques that I share with you in the next few chapters would become irrelevant if you haven't defined your target with precision. There's a reason why I structure my videos, book, communication, e-mails, websites in a certain way. You would realise that it is the same way that successful companies structure their communication. The first step to growing your business fast is to define your ideal client. Make sure you do this before you move on the next two chapters. The hidden benefit of doing this right will be the effortless ability to communicate to your target with clarity and attract them to you and your brand, making it easier for you to reach more people with your business.

Chapter 3: Never Lose a Sale

This chapter covers your business Trap, the second step in the Fast Business Growth system. I trust that you have defined your ideal customer and you have gone out and found what it is your ideal customers you are looking for. If you have done so, this chapter will be great for you. Everything flows very fast and easily when the research on the Target is done. Your Trap answers the questions such as "How can I offer the most profitable product? How can I capture more leads with the same effort? How can I maximise the conversions of leads into sales?"

In many cases, having the right profitable offer and maximising sales from existing exposure can double, triple or more your business results. Thus, when it comes to growing your business fast, you want to set up your trap right. The best way to do this is online.

Remember that you can spend your one on one time with customers physically that is limited by your time, energy, and location. Or you can have an online version of you selling for you 24/7. I believe the latter is more effective. Online systems are scalable, use less of your time and effort and most importantly while your online version of you is selling and building your business, you give yourself time that you can spend time on things that matter, like your actual client work, your family, your passion whatever else you want to do in life.

Here are the 3 things you need to remember about setting up the right trap:

1. An irresistible offer
2. An online presence that generates leads
3. A sales process that turns leads into paying customers

An Irresistible Offer

When you want to think of an offer that you can provide to your ideal customer, ask yourself, "What can I give my ideal customer if he or she was willing to pay me for what I was worth, for everything that I have?" Essentially, what would be your highest level offer which can create the greatest results for your ideal customer? This would be the starting point of your trap. A method that works when deciding what price to charge for your product or service, is to look at how much value you are creating for your customer.

Use the currencies of money, time and emotion when you do this. How much money are you making or saving them? How much time are you saving them? How much positive emotion can you create for them or how much painful emotion can you save them? The greater you can quantify your value with these currencies, the more valuable your product and the higher you can charge. Your target is to come up with an irresistible offer for your ideal client, something they cannot refuse when presented in front of them. The region is normally 10 times and above for people to drop their resistance to buying. Getting your offer tweaked to its most profitable potential alone, in some cases, can create 10 times results in a business. The principle to remember here is the bigger the problem you solve, the more you can charge and the more profitable your business can be.

An Online Presence That Generates Leads

Most websites are structured in a way that it does not make money for the business owner. You know this kind of website, 5 pages: Home, About, Services, Products, Contact Us. These sites, no matter how pretty, don't produce results or financial return for the owners, and I don't recommend them to you. What you want are single action sites which offer something valuable to your ideal customers. Typically this value is in the form of educational information, which provide insight to the customer on their problem, their ideal solution, and how to act. This information alone, is very valuable. The best part of the information being online is that it can educate your customer for you 24/7 without you being there. Imagine the introduction and education that you do every single time you meet a new customer, who you are and who your company is, what problem you solve, what criteria should be used for the customer to make the best decision, and what your offer is. Take all of that information and now put it into your online presence.

A simple but extremely effective lead generator (FastBusinessGrowth.co/MediaCheatSheet)

This is a great example of leverage, where you create everything once, and it can be consumed by 1, 100, or 100,000 people in a short span of time. The last part that pulls this online presence together is that the most valuable information is given to the customer only after they give you their name and contact details, thus allowing you to build a customer list and thereafter build a relationship with them by sending them more information by e-mail, calling them, connecting them with your social media assets, or giving them freebies, discounts or vouchers. This online presence is the one thing that you need to have as a centrepiece of your brand, to funnel all your exposure, word of mouth, goodwill, advertisements, traffic, events, to, and this converts your hustle into a hungry list of potential clients waiting to pay you for your services. There are many ways you can create systems that create an effective online presence for you - my most valuable advice is to not build anything from scratch. Many existing, highly effective and value for money options exist, do your research or get a trusted referral.

<u>A Sales Process That Turns Leads Into Paying Customers</u>

The last element of an effective Trap for your business is to have a sales process that turns leads into paying customers. There is no one way to do this, in fact many different businesses use one or more ways. Some of these are:

- Online sales pages
- Online live chats
- Webinars
- Sales calls
- Face to face sales consultations
- Events
- One time offers
- Upsells and cross sells

Putting everything from the beginning of the system until now together, in the sales process you will need:

1. A specific target
2. Educating the target on their big problem they are facing
3. Giving the target a scenario of the ideal solution
4. Provide a viable action step with your irresistible offer

To add the cherry on the top of this sales process, your call to action at the end needs to create urgency and scarcity. Examples of this is a 50% discount which lasts for the next 15 minutes, or a sponsorship of $500 for the first 5 people accepted into the program.

To know which type of sales processes work best for your business and product is simple: test. Based on your target, always test people's response to mechanisms as early and as fast as possible. You don't want to make business decisions theoretically, but with actual market feedback. You also don't want to beat down a path which is a dead end, so be ready to be flexible with your approach, take feedback, and tweak your approach fast.

One word of warning, don't try to build 10 different websites with 20 different products trying 50 different sales mechanisms. This will take too much of the limited time, energy and money you have. What you want to do is focus on one Target and one Trap first, and make sure it's profitable. Once it is, then you can add on to it, you can change it up and you can expand it or build other traps for other products. But before that, it's time to take your Trap to your Target. It's the magic of Traffic coming next, because everything is now laid out and ready to reach a massive number of people. Make sure you spend the minimum amount of time to create your Trap which is able to do the things described in this chapter, before you move on into the next. I'll see you there.

Chapter 4: Never Run Out of Leads

We have come to the last step in the Fast Business Growth system, Traffic. Traffic answers the question which business owners ask like "How can I get more attention for my business?", "How can I find more customers?", "What is the most effective way to generate leads?", and "How do I use social media and ads to generate leads?"

Remember, at this point you already have a two things: Firstly, you have your Target: an ideal client defined, and you understand what they are looking for. Secondly, you have your Trap: an irresistible offer for your target, an online presence that funnels exposure into leads, and a sales process that turns leads into paying customers. Now it's time to feed this machine the fuel it needs to grow: Traffic.

Clients that spend 12 months with me execute multiple proven ways to get more traffic for their business which I have used time and again successfully. In this chapter, I will introduce 5 of them.

1. <u>Organic Social Media Posts</u>

   The first method is by using free social media traction. Your target most likely has a Facebook, Youtube, Instagram, LinkedIn, Periscope or Snapchat account. He or she also will likely be using Google, and reading from specific websites online. What you need to do with your profile is to set yourself up as an expert in your industry. How you do this is to build authority and consistency for yourself.

   One, you must educate, and show your expertise in your market, so that you are seen as an authority. Give them examples, case studies, frameworks, insights and experiences, and show them from these content pieces, and your own story, why you are the only logical choice to solve their problems. Your educational posts should educate your target on their problem, the ideal solution, and why if they don't choose your products or services, they would end up spending more time, money and energy to solve their problems themselves.

Secondly, you need to be consistent in getting your message out to the market. This would involve daily planning, daily videos, regular e-mails to your list, and curating and sharing articles, resources and links which are relevant to your audience. Consolidate the focus of all these posts and communication towards your traps - your website and public profiles.

Consistency in action is extremely important as people want to know that you are here to stay and not disappear. Huge online brands, whether entrepreneurs like Gary Vaynerchuk or Grant Cardone, to this day, are posting at least 8 times a day on all their different platforms. Beyond volume of activity, your content needs to have a few factors, one is the 'wow' factor, where you showcase something that your audience wants, or would admire. An example is a real estate agent showing videos of walkthroughs of amazing homes to their following. Another factor is the 'now' factor, where what you share is happening real-time or is relevant in the here and now, and not outdated. People want to follow someone who's an expert and using methods that work right now, not yesterday - and want to see that you are authentic with being in the moment. People have started trusting brands who are raw and in the moment more, compared to brands who spend lots of resources and time on post editing to make a piece of content look slick. Due to this, live streaming - whether in a video, an image or text, has become a huge way brands deliver and consumers consume content.

Being consistent, 'wow'-ing them and showing them what works 'now', gives you the authority and consistency that your audience needs to trust you and take the step towards working with you. Using this method, small business brands have been built to hundreds of thousands of followers and millions of views on content, without a single dollar of advertising, in less than a year! You need to understand where people's attention is going, and what platforms you can leverage for maximum effect, and you can achieve huge leverage on your content.

2. Online Paid Advertising

The second method, using paid advertising, is one of the most powerful methods that you can use right now to grow your business. This method means using a budget where you put in money for advertising on the internet, to generate leads. You can do this in many different platforms, such as Facebook or Google. My personal preference is using Facebook. The reason for this is that I can specifically choose my target demographic based on the target client, which we defined earlier in the book.

Using specific demographics means a few things - one, that you reach out to the right audience, two, that your message reaches the right people in less time, and three, your message reaches them with less of your effort and money. In fact, if you know how to run pay-per-click (PPC) advertising well, as it is known in the industry, you can generate leads to your site, at a low price. As an example, I've driven qualified leads for as low as 10 cents. This is probably less than the cost of printing a flyer or making a cold call, which are traditional and resource-intensive methods of generating leads.

Think about how much it would cost for you, and how much time it would take, to physically go and find a qualified lead, whether it is using flyers, sales agents, telemarketing and other traditional methods. Now, think about the physical alternative of meeting them in your office, home or outside over coffee and spending 1 hour with them to share with them what you would share with every single time.

I would like you to recognise a few things here. For the price of hiring or contracting a salesperson, you would easily be able to drive thousands of leads to your Trap (website and assets) and engage with qualified customers. Now, here's where it gets real exciting. With online paid traffic, you can scale up the number of leads you generate, without increasing the time and effort put in. This means by increasing your budget by 100%, you can increase the number of leads you generate by 100%, without spending any additional time or effort, because the setup time for each advertising campaign is exactly the same. This has enormous implications for productivity and profit in your business. If you didn't have to talk to 10 times the number of people and go for 10 times the number of meetings in order to generate 10 times the leads in your business, how much more profitable could you be? How much more time would you gain?

This is really, really, important, especially if you're going all out with your time and the resources, and the energy to grow your business. I highly recommend using this method as the backbone of traffic generation. If you're not already proficient at online marketing, find the best consultant or coach that you know to either do it for you or guide you in a very focused way, so you save time and don't waste money on ineffective campaigns.

Like every other aspect of business, you need to test and measure. I typically run at least 2 to 4 different ads for any given campaign, which I then test for the conversion rate and price per click. I stick to the highest converting ones, and then create new ones to test and improve the results even more. Using these methods our campaigns consistently get to the top 10% to top 1% of Facebook advertisers. Before you set out with your campaigns, it is important to know your ideal client really intimately, to know who they are, what kind of content they read, the personalities, publications and pages they like, so you can be specific with your targeting. Running advertisements with generic marketing language to an undefined target audience is almost the same as throwing away your cash out the window!

3. Partnerships

The next method on the list is partnerships. Find people who are already reaching your target audience, who have a client list already. People, brands, celebrities, companies, organisations probably exist that meet this criteria, and are probably doing their own thing. As long as what you and these potential partners market do not conflict or directly compete, it is likely you can find a way to partner with them. In many cases, just being able to give value to someone's client list with meaningful insights alone is enough value to these potential partners.

For other potential partners, you may work out a profit-sharing arrangement. For example, out of the revenue that you get through a partnership, the partner can receive anywhere between 10% to 50% of the sale, which are typical numbers in the marketing industry. In general, the more effort, input and value partners bring in, the more profit they would expect in the arrangement.

Using partnerships, I have been invited to events and featured in partners' online campaigns and events. This allowed me to share my brand and insights to other audiences beyond my reach. This method can work especially well for you if you find and forge partnerships with celebrities and thought leaders in their respective fields or markets who have a large and engaged following.

As a marketing partner myself for other product owners and service providers, I have been able to also firstly add value to my list with educational content from credible product owners, and also importantly been able to monetise my client list more.

4. Meetups

Simple but powerful connections with people through meeting up!

This is something close to me because I do love to meet people. It is always great to be part of a community, and

Meetup is an online platform where you can find like-minded people wanting the same thing. When you pay (almost nothing) for an admin account, you're able to create multiple communities. Within half a year, our network of communities across 6 cities in southeast Asia grew to more than 3,000 people organically.

The secret to having attractive Meetup groups is to have a good name that attracts your target, as well as compelling events where people can gain valuable insights and make meaningful connections with like-minded people. Wherever we go, even if it is for a casual social gathering, we could expect at least a dozen people to attend. If you create a compelling event with great value, you can have far more, and it becomes a great way to generate leads and buzz with little to no money.

5. Free Media Exposure

Getting into the media in the past 3 years with our businesses taught me a lot. It gave us a lot of credibility, a lot of partnerships, and attention. We have been featured more than 30 times, online and offline, on television, radio, newspapers, magazines, regional conferences, and online platforms, and as a result, getting in front of hundreds of thousands of people and positioning us as an authority in our field, at zero cost.

The ability to get into the media means you get a great opportunity to present yourself as an authority in your industry and it allows other people to get to know about you and your story. They will be interested to find out more about you and they will start searching for your content, your previous achievements and your articles. Many of them will start to contact you for partnerships and other opportunities. The media is also a powerful tool to position yourself or your brand. As an example, I showcased the fact that I have been featured on more than 12 media platforms ranging from TV, radio, newspaper, to online and regional events. This gives significant credibility to me and my brand, and very quickly answers the questions in a potential client's head: "Can I trust this person? Is he credible?" When you are featured in the media, the conclusion is most likely yes, because you have been featured and therefore have been subject to media and public scrutiny. Therefore, they can now trust you.

The key point in all of this is that every media outlet is different. Each media outlet has a specific audience that they engage, with a particular editorial philosophy and criteria. It is important to understand that people in the media are also humans, with biases, limited attention spans, and primarily have a concern of the sustainability of their job and the platform, so they will look for stories which serve these purposes.

Regardless of medium or journalist, the number one thing they look for is a good story. Nobody's interested in your company, product or service. However, they are interested in a riveting story of an underdog, or a story of redemption, or a 'David versus Goliath story' in an industry. Think about the story you tell about your brand, your business or your personal story that would be interesting for a media platform and the audience they serve, then craft that story from that perspective.

After generating so many success stories using the media, I actually put together a free cheat sheet of how you can use the media for free exposure for your business. This gives you the ability to create leads, position yourself as an authority, and charge more for products and services. If you'd like to know more just click on the link below.
http://FastBusinessGrowth.co/MediaCheatSheet

6. Guest Speaking

When you become an expert in a particular area, people and organisations start coming to you for advice and opinions on things. Guest speaking is one of the ways that you can get your brand your content out there and people can get to know about you.

This is similar to partnerships where you position yourself as an expert to someone else's organisation or audience. As a guest speaker, you can educate and provide valuable content and insights to the audience live at an event, or even on online webinars or guest posts. Live events provide a special kind of connection and whether you speak to 20 people or 2,000 people in a room, the more you speak, the more people who are your target audience would connect with you and want to know more. Nurtured the right way, it will be able to become a steady stream of leads for your business.

Perhaps you are afraid of public speaking, or you may think that you have nothing interesting to say. The art of speaking and talking to an audience is something that I could write a whole book about. What you need to know right now, however, is that you are enough. You have a great story which is unique that your ideal target customer will love you for.

Model stories of great leaders and orators, so you have it into a neat presentation, including the problem that you solve, the type of people that you help, and examples of your services. Remember the source of every business is always personal, so share what personally brought you to where you are with your business, how you got started, and why you are doing it.

When you have your story lined out, practice, and practice, and practice your story. Remember what I said about being an authority - consistency. This is something that you need to be so that you become proficient and be seen as an authority, go to guy in your industry.

The more chances you seize to speak as a guest in events, seminars and any other platform, the more exposure and opportunities you get outside of it. As an example, from one guest speaking event with less than 30 people in the room, I was roped in for two other media interviews on radio and television, recorded a live video to post on social media and I received more than 5 leads for my business that same day. All for 45 minutes of talking time.

All these methods are used to generate massive traffic for any business and that is the last step in the Fast Business Growth system. If you execute these strategies in a very focused, efficient and effective way, you will be able to take any business and double it or add six figures into it in under 12 months just as my businesses, my clients and my peers in the industry. The only thing that you need right now is to go and put it all together.

Chapter 5: No More Inefficiencies in Your Business

If you talk to any entrepreneur, the vision of success in his or her head is never about working 24/7 or having burnout. However, a huge problem that I see with entrepreneurs who are struggling is that they end up working all the time. They are constantly firefighting in their business, chasing new clients, servicing customers, pulling together the team and trying to keep the ship afloat, and it never seems there is enough time to get things done, let alone scale up the business. The one thing the entrepreneur's need to do to buy back the time, and therefore, their life, is to create systems, processes and having the right team in the right place doing the right thing so that things just get done without taking up the entrepreneur's time disproportionately. In fact, when in practice, the entrepreneur sees more results while working less. When this happens, entrepreneurs go from being self employed to being a business owner, from overwork to working half the time and from firefighting, to freedom.

When you want to create a business system for yourself so that you can work less and achieve more with your business, you want to start by looking at what your genius is. It is likely that you are really good in one or two areas in your business but not the rest. The one or two things which you are great at, you need to continue doing and increase doing, because this creates the most value, profit, and joy for you. The things which you are not good at, you need to create processes to eliminate, minimise, delegate or automate, in that order. Many business owners make the fatal mistake of trying to hire staff and teach them what they are good at. However, this creates more problems because the aspects of the business which are already being neglected, get neglected even more. Complications arise and businesses fail as a result.

If you are good at sales, then you want to have an assistant who is able to handle all the client paperwork, billing, and communication with the client for delivery, so that you can focus on selling and bringing in clients. If you are great at teaching, coaching or consulting, then you will want to find the right team, partners or vendor you can create or customize the right technology platform to put all your intellectual property on.

As with many other business mistakes, many entrepreneurs do not focus on the top things that will make a difference in this area. The purpose of a system is to remove work, streamline processes, and buy back time for the entrepreneur while maintaining or increasing results in the business. Some mistakes that I see all the time include investing in complex systems which do not fit the needs of the business, or hiring staff who make systemisation more difficult, rather than easier.

The first thing I would do in a business immediately is to take out the lower value activities. For example, I would hire a trusted and value-for-money accountant or service provider to handle all the administrative people off of this year and integrate a cloud Accounting Service like Xero or ReceiptBank so that I do not have to think about how to put an accounting system together, let alone manage it.

When you are looking at systemising your business, think of these questions to decide which areas to systemise first, and the approach:

- What areas frustrate me the most right now?
- What are the lowest value activities that I repeatedly have to devote time and energy to?
- What solution or provider exists which can do this for me?
- What do I keep, eliminate, reduce, delegate and automate?

As with any effort, taking consistent steps is key. Automating just one process may seem tiny compared to the seemingly never-ending list of things on your mind, however keeping at it and building your system piece by piece over time will snowball and when done well, you will have a well-oiled machine which removes the key frustrations in your business from you, while giving you more time to focus on even more growth and impact.

Chapter 6: The Rocket is Launching... Are You Ready?

In truth, what you need to grow your business and explode by 6 figures in the next 12 months have been laid out for you in this book. This is accessible to everyone and I don't care who you are, where you're from, what labels, titles, certificates you have or don't have. You can launch your rocket now. In my growth and my journey, I have realized that you really only need two things, number one, the strategy. This book has laid them out for you. There are many ways for you to get more strategies or even have a chat with me to work out the finer details of your business strategy in the next 12 months. The second thing is the mindset and faith in yourself that you can achieve these results. If you don't have them, if you can't see this happening for yourself, you will never take the first step. You'll always find yourself doing things halfheartedly and without conviction. You will never get there.

If you find yourself questioning whether you can do it or not, whether you have the ability, skills, talent resources or the willpower or you're missing something, I want to share with you what my mentor once shared with me: You can do it. You are worth so much more than you know. I believe in you. If you're alive and reading this right now then you have the talent. You have what it takes. The only thing left is to decide to come into your inspirational future and move. Fast. Unconditionally. Know that as your friend on this journey, I unconditionally believe in you, love you and I am your number one fan. It is far more important to act from a place of love because the other option is to act from fear disguised as practicality. Love moves me to do things far beyond my comfort zone and it will for you too. My love for my family - my wife and my unborn child, drives me every single day, even on days I feel down, sick, demotivated or anything other than outstanding. Find your unconditional love and you will find your success.

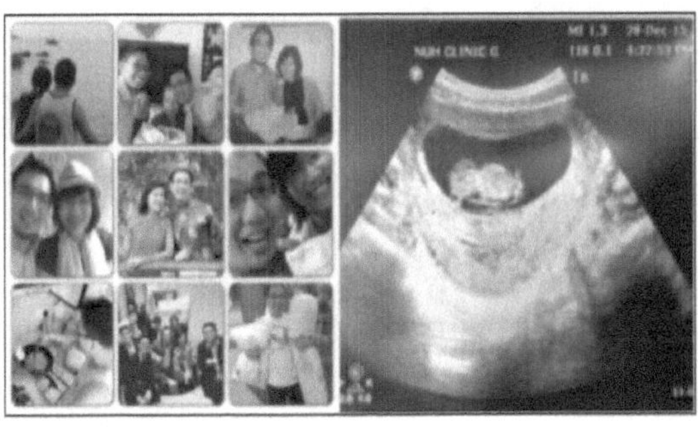

The love that drives me

It's important to start and to start now. What I would like to offer you is the ability to have self-awareness. That's the start for meaningful action. So let's do it again. Where do you stand in Target, Trap and Traffic? 10 being absolutely perfect and no improvement is needed, and 1 meaning you have absolutely no clue. Being honest with yourself and scoring yourself on these 3 steps will give you a starting point for a plan to grow your business.

Self - Diagnosis

TARGET	? / 10
TRAP	? / 10
TRAFFIC	? / 10

Where does your business stand? Start now.

To empower you on the journey and constantly reinforce these lessons,I would like to give you three gifts. However, these gifts will only serve you if you decide to go unconditionally into your head, your mission, and your purpose. Adding six figures to your business is not about the money. It is about your life. Your impact. Your purpose. It is about the people that you are able to help, the families that you are able to feed, and the legacy that you can leave behind. So, treat these gifts with utmost respect because they are invaluable and just using this gifts alone is more than enough to give you the boost you need to start on this journey of growth.

Firstly, you need a community to launch a rocket. This would include mentors, a team, an inner circle of peers and partners and supporters who are on the same path and understand your journey. Having a community is a HUGE help because most people outside do not understand the journey. As a bonus, I would like to invite you to our private global business owner community on Facebook, Get Your Business To $1 Million. You will find friends, partners, people who are just a few steps ahead of where you are and people that you can help and inspire. These people come from all over the world, have a heart to help and a drive to grow.

Join here: https://www.facebook.com/groups/GetYourBizToOneMillion/

Get Your Business To $1M Private Business Owner Community

The second bonus has to do with you being the pilot of your rocket. To get there, you need to focus on your one destination. The ability to focus on the ONE big thing and to channel your strengths into your day to day work is a game changer for any entrepreneur who feels overwhelmed, stretched too thin, and dealing with too many things which are not worth your time or in your domain of expertise. You can grab a one to one clarity call with me to identify exactly the best strategy and fastest path to your business growth in the next 12 months. I normally charge $750 for 1 hour of consultation, but because you have read this book right until this point, I am giving it to you at no charge. I only seek your commitment to attend and be fully present during the call, so we make the most of our time and not take time away from other people I can help.

www.ingramcontent.com/pod-product-compliance
Lightning Source LLC
LaVergne TN
LVHW040934150826
845672LV00007B/2352

* 9 7 9 8 4 7 1 5 7 3 3 1 4 *